The Old-Time Radio Trivia Book

by Mel Simons

The Old-Time Radio Trivia Book

by Mel Simons

BearManor Media
2004

Dedication

*This book is dedicated to Frances Simons,
Maralyn and Bernie Goldman,
and Roberta Oriel*

Mel Simons

Acknowledgements

This book is possible because of the old-time radio stars themselves. Legends like Jack Benny, Eddie Cantor, and Fred Allen filled my youth with hours of wondrous listening, and many later corresponded with me and sent me the autographed photos you see in this book.

I thank those who gave me the opportunity to talk about old-time radio *on* the radio and television as a regular on their shows:

PAUL BENZAQUIN SHOW (1 year – WNAC TV & WHDH Radio, Boston)

GOOD DAY SHOW (4 years – WCVB TV, Boston, Betty Levin, Producer)

JOE FRANKLIN SHOW (3 years – WOR TV, New York)

The three legends of WBZ Radio in Boston

LARRY GLICK (14 years)

BOB RALEIGH (6 years)

STEVE LeVEILLE (5 years and still counting)

Foreword

Mel Simons has become an institution on late night radio in Boston. For more than 25 years he has entertained listeners with trivia quizzes based on his unique and massive collection of recorded sound. From the earliest recordings of presidents and celebrities to the most recent TV theme songs, Mel includes something for everyone.

Central to his collection and closest to his heart is radio. If Mel had been born a few decades earlier he might have been a radio actor or a member of the studio orchestra. But fortunately for us his calling has been to collect the sounds and memorabilia of the era known as the Golden Days of Radio. Mel's life-long desire to gather and preserve artifacts of this important part of American cultural history has led to the creation of this fun book.

Share this book with a relative or friend or curl up in your favorite chair and enjoy your own personal quiz show. It will make you smile as you see the names of actors, characters and places that have been a part of your life since you first heard them on the radio long ago. It may make you laugh out loud as you recall people, shows, songs and even commercials you thought you had forgotten.

Return with Mel Simons now to "those thrilling days of yesteryear" in The Old-Time Radio Trivia Book.

– Steve LeVeille
WBZ Boston

Quiz #1

Match the Announcer with the program.
(Answers on page 113)

1. Fibber McGee & Molly
2. Jack Benny
3. Romance of Helen Trent
4. Kraft Music Hall
5. Arthur Godfrey
6. Aunt Jenny
7. The Lone Ranger
8. Amos & Andy
9. Your Hit Parade
10. Little Orphan Annie

a. Tony Marvin
b. Andre Baruch
c. Ken Carpenter
d. Harlow Wilcox
e. Don Wilson
f. Pierre Andre
g. Bill Hay
h. Fielden Farrington
i. Dan Seymour
j. Fred Foy

Jimmy Durante

Quiz #2

Match the saying with the person.
(Answers on page 113)

1. "Goodnight, Mrs. Callabash, wherever you are!"
2. "I know many things, for I walk by night!"
3. "How do you do!"
4. "Wanna buy a duck?"
5. "Heigh Ho Everybody!"
6. "Dear Mama Mia…"
7. "What a revoltin' development this is!"
8. "Howdy Bub!"
9. "You Hoo! Is Anybody?"
10. "Good evening, Mr. & Mrs. North & South America…"

a. Molly Goldberg
b. Chester A. Riley
c. Rudy Vallee
d. The Whistler
e. Jimmy Durante
f. Joe Penner
g. The Mad Russian
h. Watler Winchell
i. Titus Moody
j. Luigi Basco

Frank Sinatra

Quiz #3

Your Hit Parade
(Answers on page 114)

From the following 15 singers:
5 appeared on the radio version of *Your Hit Parade*
5 appeared on the television version of *Your Hit Parade*
5 appeared on neither

1. Snooky Lanson
2. Frank Sinatra
3. Eddie Fisher
4. Patti Page
5. Dorothy Collins
6. Tommy Leonetti
7. Frankie Laine
8. Andy Russell
9. Dick Haymes
10. Doris Day
11. Giselle McKenzie
12. Russell Arms
13. Dinah Shore
14. Joan Edwards
15. Kitty Kallen

Eve Arden
Our Miss Brooks

Quiz #4

Commercials
(Answers on page 114)

Fill in the product:

1. The big red letters stand for the _____ family.
2. Get _____ _____ _____, Charlie.
3. What'll you have? _____ _____ _____.
4. _____ _____ for your breakfast, starts the day off shining bright.
5. _____ does everything.
6. Take soothing _____ _____ and feel good again.
7. Call for _____ _____.
8. _____ _____ hits the spot, 12 full ounces, that's a lot.
9. _____ really stops B.O.!
10. Laugh a while, let a song be your smile, use _____ _____.

Jack Benny and Fred Allen

Quiz #5

Jack Benny
(Answers on page 115)

1. Who sang "Pickle in the middle and the mustard on top?"
2. What band leader replaced Phil Harris?
3. Where did Jack meet Mary Livingston?
4. Who did Dennis Day replace as the show's vocalist?
5. What was the name of the quartet that sang "HMMMM?"
6. What was the name of the man that guarded Jack's safe?
7. Who was Jack's violin teacher?
8. What kind of a car did Jack drive?
9. Who played Rochester?
10. What two famous sponsors did Jack have?

Roy Rogers

Quiz #6

Match the horse with its owner.
(Answers on page 115)

1. Hopalong Cassidy
2. Roy Rogers
3. Gene Autry
4. Bobby Benson
5. The Long Ranger
6. Tonto
7. The Cisco Kid
8. Dale Evans
9. Sergeant Preston
10. Tom Mix

a. Trigger
b. Tony
c. Amigo
d. Buttermilk
e. Rex
f. Topper
g. Silver
h. Champion
i. Diablo
j. Scout

Quiz #7

Match the theme song with the show.
(Answers on page 115)

1. Red River Valley
2. Thanks for the Memory
3. When Irish Eyes Are Smiling
4. Love Nest
5. William Tell Overture
6. Friendship
7. When the Moon Comes over the Mountain
8. April Showers
9. Seems Like Old Times
10. Polly Wolly Doodle

a. George Burns & Gracie Allen
b. Our Gal Sunday
c. Kate Smith
d. Bob Hope
e. Al Jolson
f. My Friend Irma
g. Just Plain Bill
h. Arthur Godfrey
i. The Lone Ranger
j. Duffy's Tavern

Quiz #8

True or False
(Answers on page 116)

1. *Your Show of Shows* was a popular radio show.
2. *The FBI in Peace and War* was later changed to *This Is Your FBI.*
3. Mel Blanc once had his own radio show.
4. Dennis Day once had his own radio show.
5. Laurel & Hardy once had their own radio show.
6. The television show *Let's Make a Deal* began on radio.
7. *Little Orphan Annie* and *Captain Midnight* both offered secret decoders as premiums.
8. Fireside chats were made popular on radio by President Harry Truman.
9. Philip Morris once sponsored Milton Berle on radio.
10. Ipana Toothpaste featured Gardol.

Marion and Jim Jordan
Fibber McGee & Molly

Quiz #9

Fibber McGee & Molly
(Answers on page 116)

1. Who played Fibber McGee & Molly?
2. Name their long-time sponsor.
3. Who was the mayor of the town?
4. Who played the mayor?
5. Fibber was constantly having a friendly feud with whom?
6. One of the most famous running gags in radio was used every week on this show. What was it?
7. What was Mr. Wimple's first name?
8. How did he refer to his wife?
9. What was the name of the little girl that used to visit Fibber?
10. Who played her?

Rudy Vallee

Quiz #10

Match the sponsor with the show.
(Answers on page 116)

1. Gangbusters
2. Ma Perkins
3. Let's Pretend
4. The FBI in Peace and War
5. Your Hit Parade
6. Big Sister
7. Morton Downey
8. House of Mystery
9. Manhattan Merry-Go-Round
10. Life Can Be Beautiful

a. Lava Soap
b. Post Cereals
c. Waterman Pens
d. Spic and Span
e. Oxydoll
f. Dr. Lyons Tooth Powder
g. Lucky Strike
h. Coca Cola
i. Cream of Wheat
j. Rinso

Willard Waterman (2nd Gildy)
The Great Gildersleeve

Quiz #11

Identify the night of the week each show was on.
(Answers on page 117)

1. Lux Radio Theatre
2. The Adventures of Sam Spade
3. Gillette Cavalcade of Sports
4. Gunsmoke
5. Fibber McGee & Molly
6. Jack Carson
7. The Lone Ranger
8. Mr. District Attorney
9. Jack Benny
10. Phil Harris-Alice Faye

Phil Harris

Quiz #12

Match the star with his sidekick.
(Answers on page 117)

1. Red Ryder
2. Colonel Stoopnagle
3. Mr. Keene
4. Cisco Kid
5. Sherlock Holmes
6. Matt Dillon
7. Wild Bill Hichok
8. Henry Morgan
9. Gene Autry
10. Kate Smith

a. Pancho
b. Mike Clancy
c. Ted Collins
d. Jingles
e. Chester
f. Pat Buttram
g. Little Beaver
h. Budd
i. Arnold Stang
j. Dr. Watson

Sheldon Leonard

Quiz #13

General Questions
(Answers on page 117)

1. Who lived on the B-Bar-B Ranch?
2. Who was the Colgate Shave Cream man?
3. Who was Chick Carter?
4. Who was the singing lady?
5. Who shouted "Call for Philip Morris!"?
6. Name the dialect comedian who told "Sam Lapidas Jokes."
7. What did David Harding do?
8. Who was Dr. Christian's nurse?
9. What program came from "the Little Theatre off Times Square"?
10. Phillips H. Lord created what famous radio show?

Quiz #14

The Lone Ranger
(Answers on page 118)

1. Who played The Lone Ranger?
2. What was The Lone Ranger's name?
3. Who played Tonto?
4. Who was The Lone Ranger's nephew?
5. Why was he called The Lone Ranger?
6. What was the name of the gang that ambushed the State Rangers?
7. Who sponsored the program?
8. What was The Lone Ranger's trademark?
9. What did he usually say to his horse?
10. Tonto often called The Lone Ranger "Kemo Sabe." What did it mean?

Quiz #15

Commercials
(Answers on page 118)

Fill in the products:

1. Brush your teeth with _____.
2. M-M-Good, M-M-Good, that's what _____ are, M-M-Good.
3. _____ is the shampoo that glorifies your hair.
4. See the U.S.A. in your _____.
5. _____ is like a doctor's prescription.
6. Ninety-nine and forty-four, one hundred percent pure, it floats, _____ _____.
7. He's feeling his _____.
8. _____ _____, the super delicious cereal!
9. _____ makes the very best.
10. _____, Breakfast of Champions.

Burt Parks

Quiz #16

True or False
(Answers on page 118)

1. Tom Mix played himself on radio.
2. Joe Frisco was a stuttering comedian.
3. Danny Thomas often appeared as a character actor on *The Lone Ranger*.
4. George Gobel often appeared as a character actor on *Tom Mix*.
5. On *Kraft Music Hall*, Oscar Levant played piano for Bing Crosby.
6. Baby Snooks originally starred Baby Rose Marie.
7. Captain Marvel was a successful radio show in the 1940's.
8. Atwater Kent was among the first to make radios.
9. Judy Garland once starred in *Meet Corliss Archer*.
10. Walter Winchell had a friendly feud with Ben Bernie.

Alice Fay

Quiz #17

Match the pet with its owner.
(Answers on page 119)

1. Little Orphan Annie's dog
2. Jack Benny's parrot
3. Sgt. Preston's dog
4. Smilin' Ed McConnell's gremlin
5. Roy Roger's dog
6. Smilin' Ed McConnell's cat
7. Buster Brown's dog
8. Blondie's dog
9. Smilin' Ed McConnell's mouse
10. Lee Duncan's dog

a. Froggie
b. King
c. Squeakie
d. Tige
e. Bullet
f. Midnite
g. Rin Tin Tin
h. Polly
i. Daisy
j. Sandy

Quiz #18

Amos & Andy
(Answers on page 119)

1. Who created and played Amos & Andy?
2. What was the Kingfish's name?
3. He was in charge of what lodge?
4. Who played the Kingfish?
5. What was the name of the Kingfish's wife?
6. What did Amos do for a living?
7. Andy's longest and most publicized romance was with whom?
8. What did the Kingfish's mother-in-law usually call him?
9. Who was the Kingfish's lawyer?
10. What was the name of the messenger boy in the lodge hall?

Quiz #19

Match the sponsor with the show.
(Answers on page 119)

1. Little Orphan Annie
2. Ed Wynn
3. Friday Night Fights
4. The Big Story
5. Just Plain Bill
6. Quick as a Flash
7. The Adventures of Sam Spade
8. Suspense
9. Wild Bill Hickock
10. Death Valley Days

a. Roma Wines
b. Gillette
c. Helbros Watches
d. Boraxo
e. Pall Mall
f. Wildroot Cream Oil
g. Kellogg's Sugar Pops
h. Ovaltine
i. Texaco
j. Whitehall Pharmacal Company

Groucho Marx

Quiz #20

Match the quiz show with its host.
(Answers on page 120)

1. You Bet Your Life
2. Juvenille Jury
3. Break the Bank
4. Queen for a Day
5. The Quiz Kids
6. Strike It Rich
7. Take It or Leave It
8. Twenty Questions
9. People Are Funny
10. Truth or Consequences

a. Joe Kelly
b. Groucho Marx
c. Bill Slater
d. Jack Barry
e. Jack Bailey
f. Phil Baker
g. Ralph Edwards
h. Art Linkletter
i. Burt Parks
j. Warren Hull

Jay Jostyn
Mr. District Attorney

Quiz #21

General Questions
(Answers on page 120)

1. Who was John J. Anthony?
2. Who created I Love a Mystery?
3. What program began with a squeaking door?
4. Who were George Shelton, Lulu McConnell, and Harry McNaughton?
5. Who played the butler on The Jack Carson Show?
6. What show did Uncle David appear on?
7. What show did Papa David appear on?
8. What were the last names of Lum & Abner?
9. What was the name of their store?
10. Where was the store located?

Bob Elliott and Ray Goulding
Bob & Ray

Quiz #22

Match the saying with the person.
(Answers on page 120)

1. Good evening from Hollywood.
2. You nasty man.
3. Heeeeeeeeeey, Abbott!
4. So long until tomorrow.
5. Yowzah, yowzah, yowzah.
6. Love dat man!
7. Ah, there's good news tonight!
8. The programs gonna be different tonight!
9. Someday, ah said, somebody knocked!
10. Aren't we devils?

a. Gabriel Heatter
b. Louella Parsons
c. Senator Claghorn
d. Joe Penner
e. Ralph Edwards
f. Ben Bernie
g. Lou Costello
h. Ed Wynn
i. Lowell Thomas
j. Beulah

Quiz #23

The Shadow
(Answers on page 121)

1. In reality, The Shadow was who?
2. Who was his lovely traveling companion?
3. How did The Shadow make himself invisible?
4. Where did he learn this?
5. When did he learn this?
6. What famous movie star once played The Shadow?
7. What was the name of the police commissioner?
8. Who was the cab driver?
9. Who sponsored *The Shadow*?
10. What did The Shadow always say at the beginning of the program?

Quiz #24

What instrument did each band leader play?
(Answers on page 121)

1. Tommy Dorsey
2. Benny Goodman
3. Harry James
4. Buddy Rich
5. Jimmy Dorsey
6. Glen Miller
7. Xavier Cugart
8. Tito Guizar
9. Vincent Lopez
10. Rudy Vallee

Penny Singleton
Blondie

Quiz #25

True or False
(Answers on page 121)

1. Guy Lombardo was once the bandleader on *Your Hit Parade*.
2. *Our Gal Sunday* preceded *The Romance of Helen Trent*.
3. Uncle Fletcher appeared on *Valiant Lady*.
4. One of boxing's earliest fights to be broadcast was the famous long count Dempsey-Tunney fight.
5. Betty Clooney was the vocalist on *Songs for Sale*.
6. Mrs. Nussbaum's first name was Pansy.
7. Albert Mitchell was The Answer Man.
8. Hopalong Cassidy's ranch was the Bar-20 Ranch.
9. Anne Elstner starred in *Portia Faces Life*.
10. Lorenzo Jones' wife was named Barbara.

Milton Berle

Quiz #26

Match the announcer was the program.
(Answers on page 122)

1. Eddie Cantor
2. Milton Berle
3. Lux Radio Theatre
4. Young Widder Brown
5. The Whistler
6. George Burns & Gracie Allen
7. Break the Bank
8. House Party
9. You Bet Your Life
10. The Shadow

a. Frank Gallop
b. George Fenneman
c. Bill Goodwin
d. George Ansboro
e. Jack Slattery
f. Andre Baruch
g. Marvin Miller
h. Bud Collier
i. John Milton Kennedy
j. Harry Von Zell

Hildegarde
The Raleigh Room

Quiz #27

Match the hit record with its vocalist.
(Answers on page 122)

1. Linda
2. Nature Boy
3. Tennessee Waltz
4. Slow Poke
5. Ghost Riders in the Sky
6. The Stein Song
7. White Christmas
8. That's My Desire
9. Marta
10. Rudolph the Red Nose Reindeer

a. Vaughn Moore
b. Bing Crosby
c. Rudy Vallee
d. Buddy Clark
e. Arthur Godfrey
f. Nat King Cole
g. Frankie Laine
h. Gene Autry
i. Patti Page
j. Arthur Tracy

Art Linkletter
People Are Funny *and* House Party

Quiz #28

Commercials
(Answers on page 122)

Fill in the product:

1. _____ taste good like a cigarette should.
2. When you see the three ring sign, ask the man for _____.
3. _____ for the smile of beauty.
4. _____ _____ for the smile of health.
5. You'll wonder where the yellow went when you brush your teeth with _____.
6. You know it's _____ _____ if it's brisk.
7. Willie the Penguin says, "Smoke _____!"
8. You owe your crowning glory to a _____ _____ _____.
9. Use _____, boom-boom, the foaming cleanser.
10. Everything's better with _____ _____ on it.

Quiz #29

Match the Jack
(Answers on page 123)

1. Who married Sadie Marks?
2. Who hung around with Henry Aldrich?
3. Who went to Hudson High?
4. Who was a quiz master?
5. Who played a detective?
6. Who was a summer replacement for Jack Benny?
7. Who was the announcer for Superman?
8. Who hung around with Doc & Reggie?
9. Who was a singer-musician?
10. Who used to say, "Hubbah, hubbah, hubbah?"

a. Jack Webb
b. Jack Paar
c. Jack Benny
d. Jack Carson
e. Jack Armstrong
f. Jackie Kelk
g. Jack Barry
h. Little Jack Little
i. Jackson Beck
j. Jack Packard

Quiz #30

The Great Gildersleeve
(Answers on page 123)

1. This show was originally a spin-off from what show?
2. Who was the original Gildersleeve?
3. Who was the second Gildersleeve?
4. What was Gildersleeve's full name?
5. Name his niece and nephew.
6. What did his nephew usually call him?
7. What was the name of the maid?
8. Who sponsored the show?
9. Who was Gildy's friend who owned a drug store?
10. What was the judge's name?

Bing Crosby

Quiz #31

Match the star with his real name.
(Answers on page 123)

1. Bing Crosby
2. Bob Hope
3. Al Jolson
4. Ish Kabibble
5. George Burns
6. Roy Rogers
7. Fred Allen
8. Jerry Lewis
9. Danny Thomas
10. Jack Benny

a. John Florence Sullivan
b. Mervyn Bogue
c. Joseph Levitch
d. Leonard Slye
e. Benny Kubelsky
f. Leslie Townes
g. Asa Yoelson
h. Amos Jacobs
i. Nathan Birnbaum
j. Harry Lillis

Les Brown
The Band of Renown

Quiz #32

Detective Questions
(Answers on page 124)

1. What was Mr. Keene known as?
2. What was the name of his assistant?
3. What was the name of Sam Spade's secretary?
4. How did she answer the phone?
5. What detective used disguises to trap criminals?
6. Who played Sgt. Joe Friday?
7. What was the name of the show?
8. What did Richard Diamond do at the end of the show?
9. Jay Jostyn played who?
10. Who was his right-hand man?

Orson Welles

Quiz #33

Fat and Thin Man
(Answers on page 124)

1. Where did The Fat Man always weigh himself?
2. What was The Fat Man's name?
3. What was The Thin Man's name?
4. What was his wife's name?
5. Both The Fat Man and The Thin Man were created by who?
6. Who played The Fat Man?
7. What musical instrument opened the show?
8. Who sponsored *The Fat Man*?
9. What was the name of The Thin Man's dog?
10. Who sponsored *The Thin Man*?

Edgar Bergen and Charlie McCarthy

Quiz #34

Match the theme song with the show.
(Answers on page 124)

1. Amos & Andy
2. Bing Crosby
3. Your Hit Parade
4. Judy Canova
5. Double or Nothing
6. Big Jon and Sparkie.
7. Jimmy Durante
8. Edgar Bergen and Charlie McCarthy
9. Myrt and Marge
10. Truth or Consequences

a. Inka Dinka Doo
b. Go to Sleepy, Little Baby
c. Three Little Words
d. Lucky Day
e. The Teddy Bear's Picnic
f. Happy Days Are Here Again
g. Poor Butterfly
h. The Perfect Song
i. Merrily We Roll Along
j. Where the Blue of the Night Meets the Gold of the Day

Quiz #35

True or False
(Answers on page 125)

1. Sgt. Preston's first name was Bill.
2. William Bendix went direct from *Life of Riley* on radio to television.
3. On *Truth or Consequences*, the walking man was Jack Benny.
4. The hostess of *The Big Show* was Tallulah Bankhead.
5. The Sons of the Pioneers sang with Gene Autry.
6. *Shell Chateau* starred Al Jolson.
7. Phil Baker played the harmonica.
8. *Gangbusters* was sponsored by Schaeffer Pens.
9. The comedy routine, "Who's on First?" was created by Olson and Johnson.
10. The "Old Timer" appeared on *The Fred Allen Show*.

Quiz #36

Match the hit record with the vocal group.
(Answers on page 125)

1. The Gypsy
2. Apple Blossom Time
3. Paper Doll
4. Tell Me Why
5. Moments to Remember
6. Ragg Mopp
7. Sincerely
8. Sh-Boom
9. Mr. Sandman
10. The Little Shoemaker

a. The Andrew Sisters
b. The McGuire Sisters
c. The Ink Spots
d. The Four Lads
e. The Chordettes
f. The Crew Cuts
g. The Gaylords
h. The Mills Brothers
i. The Four Aces
j. The Ames Brothers

Quiz #37

The Green Hornet
(Answers on page 125)

1.   In reality The Green Hornet was who?
2.   What was his profession?
3.   What was the name of his secretary?
4.   What identifying mark did The Green Hornet always leave?
5.   What was the Hornet's automobile called?
6.   Who was the Hornet's faithful valet?
7.   What was his ancestry?
8.   Who worked for the newspaper that had an Irish brogue?
9.   What was The Green Hornet's theme song?
10. What did the newsboy always yell at the conclusion of the program?

Quiz #38

Match the bandleader with his catch phrase.
(Answers on page 126)

1. Guy Lombardo
2. Les Brown
3. Bob Crosby
4. Spike Jones
5. Kay Kaiser
6. Glen Gray
7. Wayne King
8. Carmen Cavallero
9. Benny Goodman
10. Shep Fields

a. City Slickers
b. The Waltz King
c. Royal Canadians
d. King of Swing
e. Band of Renown
f. Rippling Rhythm
g. Casa Loma Orchestra
h. Bob Cats
i. The Poet of the Piano
j. College of Musical Knowledge

Gale Gordon

Quiz #39

Match the residence.
(Answers on page 126)

1. Black Swan Hall
2. 77 Wistful Vista
3. 212-A West 87th St., New York
4. In a shoe
5. Metropolis
6. 1313 Blueview Terrace
7. Chicago
8. 221B Baker Street
9. Summerfield
10. In the little house halfway up in the next block

a. Chester A. Riley
b. Vic and Sade
c. Fibber McGee & Molly
d. Buster Brown's dog
e. The Great Gildersleeve
f. Luigi Basco
g. Ellery Queen
h. Sherlock Holmes
i. Superman
j. Our Gal Sunday

Quiz #40

Soap Operas
(Answers on page 126)

1. What did Ma Perkins do for a living?
2. In *Just Plain Bill*, what was Bill's profession?
3. What long-running soap opera did Mary Jane Higby star in?
4. Where did *Our Gal Sunday* originally come from?
5. Who were Anne & Frank Hummert?
6. Who was Helen Trent's boyfriend?
7. What soap opera star was a cookie inventor?
8. In *Portia Faces Life*, what was Portia's profession?
9. Who told *Real Life Stories*?
10. In *John's Other Wife*, what was John's last name?

Quiz #41

Match the husband with his wife.
(Answers on page 127)

1. Phil Harris
2. Goodman Ace
3. Fred Allen
4. Ronald Coleman
5. Eddie Cantor
6. Henry Barbour
7. John Bickerson
8. Peter Lind Hayes
9. Frank Crumit
10. Ozzie Nelson

a. Portland Hoffa
b. Ida
c. Harriet Hilliard
d. Jane
e. Alice Faye
f. Julia Sanderson
g. Blanche
h. Benita Hume
i. Mary Healey
j. Fanny

Henry Morgan

Quiz #42

Commercials
(Answers on page 127)

Fill in the product:

1. _____ is the one beer to have when you're having more than one.
2. _____, America's favorite food drink.
3. You get a lot to light with a _____.
4. _____ _____, a little dab'll do ya.
5. Fight headache three ways, _____ _____.
6. _____ _____ means fine tobacco.
7. I love the tiny little tea leaves in _____ ___.
8. _____ in, dirt's out.
9. Nothing in America cleans painted walls, woodwork and linoleum like _____ _____ _____.
10. For a breakfast you can't beat, try _____ _____ _____.

Hal Peary (1st Gildy)
The Great Gildersleeve

Quiz #43

Match the saying with the person.
(Answers on page 127)

1. Is everybody happy?
2. Well, Portland, gee whiz.
3. Roll, thunder, roll.
4. Leapin' lizards.
5. Elementary, my dear Watson.
6. Hello, everybody.
7. You call me, Papa?
8. Vas you dere, Charlie?
9. So help me, I'll mow ya down.
10. Time marches on!

a. Sherlock Holmes
b. Little Orphan Annie
c. Baron Munchhausen
d. Charlie McCarthy
e. Red Ryder
f. Rosa
g. Kate Smith
h. Westbrook Van Voorhis
i. Fred Allen
j. Ted Lewis

George Burns

Quiz #44

Match the sponsor with the show.
(Answers on page 128)

1. Jack Armstrong
2. Ozzie and Harriet
3. Rudy Vallee
4. Captain Midnight
5. George Burns and Gracie Allen
6. Gene Autry
7. Pepper Young's Family
8. Aunt Jenny
9. Eddie Cantor
10. Sgt. Preston

a. Wheaties
b. Ovaltine
c. Spry
d. International Silver
e. Fleischmann's
f. Camay
g. Pabst Blue Ribbon
h. Doublemint Gum
i. Quaker Puffed Wheat and Quaker Puffed Rice
j. Maxwell House

Quiz #45

Baby Snooks
(Answers on page 128)

1. Who played Baby Snooks?
2. Who did Baby Snooks originally star with?
3. What was the original name of the show?
4. What was Snooks' last name?
5. Who played Snooks' daddy?
6. What was daddy's name?
7. What was mommy's name?
8. What was Snooks' brother's name?
9. What was unusual about the way he talked?
10. What was the show's theme song?

Quiz #46

Musical Questions
(Answers on page 128)

1. Name the singing star of *Harvest of Stars*.
2. Guy Lombardo's brother was a featured vocalist with the band. Name him.
3. Guy Lombardo's brother-in-law was a featured vocalist with the band. Name him.
4. What two famous bands did Frank Sinatra sing with?
5. What was Fred Waring's ensemble know as?
6. Who was known as the Street Singer?
7. What musical show was on opposite *The Fred Allen Show*?
8. Name the female vocalist of this show.
9. What were Billy Jones & Ernie Hare known as?
10. Who sang "That's What I Like About the South"?

Bob Hope

Quiz #47

Identify the night of the week each show was on.
(Answers on page 129)

1. Arthur Godfrey's Talent Scouts
2. The Shadow
3. You Bet Your Life
4. Red Skelton
5. Casey, Crime Photographer
6. The Green Hornet
7. Fred Allen
8. Voice of Firestone
9. Bob Hope
10. My Friend Irma

Quiz #48

Match the Bob
(Answers on page 129)

1.   Who was sponsored by Camel Cigarettes?
2.   Who's brother likes Minute Maid Orange Juice?
3.   Who played the Bazooka?
4.   Who was partners with Ray Goulding?
5.   Who rode a golden palomino?
6.   Who was a big band vocalist?
7.   Who played Archie Andrews?
8.   Who starred in *Father Knows Best*?
9.   Who created *Believe It or Not*?
10. Who worked with Jerry Colonna?

a.   Bob Hope
b.   Bobby Benson
c.   Bob Burns
d.   Bob Hastings
e.   Bob Eberly
f.   Bob Young
g.   Bob Elliott
h.   Bob Hawk
i.   Bob Ripley
j.   Bob Crosby

Quiz #49

Superman
(Answers on page 129)

1. Who played Superman?
2. Where did Superman originally come from?
3. What had the power to render Superman helpless?
4. Clark Kent worked for what newspaper?
5. Who was the editor of the newspaper?
6. Who was the girl reporter?
7. Who was the boy reporter?
8. What was Superman more powerful than?
9. Who sponsored *Superman*?
10. Where did Clark Kent usually change his clothes?

George Fenneman and Groucho Marx
You Bet Your Life

Quiz #50

Match the bandleader with his theme song.
(Answers on page 130)

1. Benny Goodman
2. Jimmy Dorsey
3. Freddie Martin
4. Guy Lombardo
5. Kay Kyser
6. Bunny Berigan
7. Glenn Miller
8. Glenn Gray
9. Tommy Dorsey
10. Bob Crosby

a. Thinking of You
b. Moonlight Serenade
c. Summertime
d. Auld Lang Syne
e. Let's Dance
f. Tonight We Love
g. Contrasts
h. Smoke Rings
i. Getting Sentimental Over You
j. I Can't Get Started

Fred Foy
Announce on The Lone Ranger

Quiz #51

True or False
(Answers on page 130)

1. Fred Allen's real name was John F. Sullivan.
2. *The Breakfast Club* once featured Johnny Desmond as vocalist.
3. Mr. District Attorney's secretary was Miss Evans.
4. Frank Sinatra starred in *Rocky Fortune*.
5. Ted Mack was the original host of the *Original Amateur Hour*.
6. Mayor Jimmy Walker of New York used to read the *Sunday Funnies* on radio.
7. The lead singer of The Ink Spots was Bill Kenny.
8. Announcer Don Wilson began his career as a sportscaster.
9. *Kukla, Fran and Ollie* was once a successful radio show.
10. *Tarzan* was once a successful radio show.

Eve Arden
Our Miss Brooks

Quiz #52

Identify the saying with the soap.
(Answers on page 130)

1. "…That because a woman is thirty-five or more, romance in life need not be over…"
2. "…The story that asks the question, can this girl from the little mining town in the West find happiness as the wife of a wealthy and titled Englishman."
3. "…The story of what it means to be the wife of a famous star."
4. "…The story of the age old conflict between a mother's duty and a woman's heart."
5. "…Dedicated to the mothers and fathers of the younger generation and to their bewildering offspring."
6. "…This tender human story of young married love is dedicated to everyone who has ever been in love."
7. "And now, smile a while with…"
8. "John Ruskin wrote this: 'Whenever money is the principal object of life, it is both ill and spent ill, and does harm both in the getting and spending. When getting and spending happiness is our aim…"

Quiz #53

Match the singing group with their first names.
(Answers on page 131)

1. McGuire Sisters
2. Ames Brothers
3. Boswell Sisters
4. DeJohn Sisters
5. Moylan Sisters
6. Mills Brothers
7. Fontaine Sisters
8. Andrews Sisters
9. DeMarco Sisters
10. Pickens Sisters

a. Patty, Maxene and LaVerne
b. Lily, Mary and Ann
c. Julie and Dux
d. Ed, Gene, Joe and Vic
e. Jane, Helen and Patti
f. Marianne, Peggy and Joan
g. Donald, Harry and Herbert
h. Dorothy, Christine and Phyllis
i. Geri, Bea and Marge
j. Connie, Vet and Martha

Quiz #54

Commercials
(Answers on page 131)

Fill in the products:

1. _____, the world's most honored watch.
2. _____, no brush, no lather, no rub in. Wet your razor then begin.
3. Lots more fun with _____ _____.
4. _____ _____, best of all king size cigarettes.
5. _____ _____: rich, rich, rich in flavor-smooth, smooth, smooth as silk.
6. It's nine o'clock - _____ watch time.
7. _____ _____ coffee: good to the last drop.
8. _____ _____ ____ _____ is that heavenly coffee.
9. Double your pleasure, double your fun with _____ ___.
10. _____ _____ cigarettes. Outstanding, and they are mild.

Norman Corwin
Writer

Quiz #55

Match the detective with his real name.

(Answers on page 131)

1. Sam Spade
2. Boston Blackie
3. Mike Barnett
4. Pat Novak
5. Sherlock Holmes
6. Nick Carter
7. Michael Shayne
8. Richard Diamond
9. Martin Kane
10. Bulldog Drummond

a. Jack Webb
b. Howard Duff
c. Dick Powell
d. Chester Morris
e. William Gargan
f. Ralph Bellamy
g. Ned Wever
h. Lon Clark
i. Basil Rathbone
j. Jeff Chandler

Lowell Thomas

Quiz #56

Multiple Choice
(Answers on page 132)

1. Who did not have his own radio show?
   a) Phil Silvers b) Clyde Beatty c) Charlie Chan

2. Who starred in *Box 13*?
   a) Paul Douglas b) Kirk Douglas c) Alan Ladd

3. Clem McCarthy is best remembered for announcing
   a) horse racing b) baseball c) football

4. Doodles Weaver was associated with what band?
   a) Kay Kyser b) Spike Jones c) Freddie Martin

5. Ellery Queen's father was known as
   a) Captain Queen b) Inspector Queen c) Colonel Queen

6. Don Winslow was in what branch of the service?
   a) Navy b) Army c) Marines

7. Molly Goldberg's friend was
   a) Mrs. Shwartz b) Mrs. Kelly c) Mrs. Bloom

8. America's Ace of the Airways was
   a) Captain Midnight b) Hop Harrigan c) Sky King

9. Ukulele Ike was
   a) Arthur Godfrey b) Bob Emery c) Cliff Edwards

10. *Escape* used to star
    a) William Gargan b) William Frawley c) William Conrad

Ralph Edwards
Truth or Consequences *and* This Is Your Life

Quiz #57

Match the hit record with its vocalist.

(Answers on page 132)

1. Anniversary Song
2. It Isn't Fair
3. That Old Black Magic
4. Because of You
5. I've Got a Lovely Bunch of Coconuts
6. Music, Music, Music
7. Come On-A-My House
8. If You Were the Only Girl
9. I Get Ideas
10. God Bless America

a. Rosemary Clooney
b. Kate Smith
c. Perry Como
d. Merv Griffin
e. Tony Bennett
f. Tony Martin
g. Billy Daniels
h. Teresa Brewer
i. Don Cornell
j. Al Jolson

Quiz #58

Our Miss Brooks
(Answers on page 132)

1. Who played Our Miss Brooks?
2. What was Miss Brooks' first name?
3. Where did she teach?
4. What subject did she teach?
5. What teacher did she have a crush on?
6. What subject did he teach?
7. He was played by what famous movie star?
8. What was the principal's names?
9. He was played by who?
10. What was the name of Miss Brooks' landlady?

Quiz #59

Match the Bill
(Answers on page 133)

1. Who was a well-known sportscaster?
2. Who was a barber?
3. Who recorded "Rock Around the Clock"?
4. Who was the lead singer of The Ink Spots?
5. Who was known as "Mr. B"?
6. Who was the M.C. of *Twenty Questions*?
7. Who played Hopalong Cassidy?
8. Who was the announcer for a famous comedy show?
9. Who created many quiz shows?
10. Who starred in *The Babe Ruth Story*?

a. Bill Stern
b. Bill Kenny
c. Bill Boyd
d. Bill Hay
e. Bill Slater
f. Just Plain Bill
g. Bill Haley
h. Bill Bendix
i. Billy Eckstine
j. Bill Todman

Don McNeill
The Breakfast Club

Quiz #60

Match the saying with the person.
(Answers on page 133)

1. Pardon me for talking in your face, Senorita!
2. The weed of crime bears bitter fruit.
3. Be good to yourself.
4. Hiya, kids...hiya, hiya...
5. Greetings from Hollywood, ladies and gentlemen.
6. Friends, and you are my friends.
7. I'm feelin' mighty low!
8. It-is-later-than-you-think.
9. Hello, folks...
10. The wheel of fortune goes round and round, and where she stops, nobody knows.

a. Candy Candido
b. Wallace Wimple
c. Ersel Twing
d. Cecil B. DeMille
e. Pedro
f. Arch Obler
g. The Shadow
h. Major Bowes
i. Don McNeil
j. Froggie the Gremlin

Bret Morrison
The Shadow

Quiz #61

Fill in the blanks
(Answers on page 133)

1. I am ____ _____, and I know many things, for I walk by night.
2. The Johnson's Wax Program with _____ _____ and _____.
3. ...Criminals and racketeers, within the law, may feel its weight by the sting of _____ _____ _____.
4. Good evening, friends. This is your host to welcome you through the creaking door into the _____ _____.
5. Hello there! We've been waiting for you. It's time to play _____ ___ _____.
6. Hello, _____ _____, where the elite meet to eat. Archie, the manager speaking...
7. _____ _____, enemy to those who make him an enemy, friend to those who have no friends.
8. Good morning _____ _____, good morning to ya...
9. Tired of the everyday routine? Ever dream of a life of romantic adventure? Want to get away from it all? We offer you _____.
10. _____, radio's outstanding theatre of thrills!

Gene Autry

Quiz #62

Match the theme song with the show.
(Answers on page 134)

1. Mr. Keene, Tracer of Lost Persons
2. Aunt Jenny's Real Life Stories
3. Lorenzo Jones
4. Eddie Cantor
5. Bob Burns
6. Gene Autry
7. Jack Benny
8. Tom Mix
9. Mr. and Mrs. North
10. The Shadow

a. I'm Back in the Saddle Again
b. Someday I'll Find You
c. Funiculi, Funicula
d. Believe Me If All Those Endearing Young Charms
e. When It's Round Up Time in Texas
f. One Hour with You
g. The Way You Look Tonight
h. The Arkansas Traveler
i. Love in Bloom
j. Omphale's Spinning Wheel

Lon Clark and Charlotte Manson
Nick Carter, Master Detective

Quiz #63

Match the parents with their kids.
(Answers on page 134)

1. Ozzie and Harriet
2. The Goldbergs
3. Vic and Sade
4. Will Brown
5. Amos Jones
6. Eddie Cantor
7. Ma Perkins
8. Phil Harris and Alice Faye
9. Fred and Mary Andrews
10. Jim and Margaret Anderson

a. Arbadella
b. Betty, Bud, Cathy
c. Rush
d. Rosalie and Sammy
e. Archie
f. Willie and Shuffle
g. Marjorie, Edna, Marilyn, Janet, Natalie
h. David and Ricky
i. Homer
j. Alice and Phyllis

Red Skelton

Quiz #64

Can You Top This
(Answers on page 134)

1. Who were the three panelists?
2. How did each panelist say hello?
3. Who created the program?
4. Who was the moderator?
5. Who told the jokes that the listening audience sent in?
6. What was the meter called that registered the studio audience's laughter?
7. What was the highest score the meter would register?
8. What was the most money a person could win?
9. What else did a person always win in addition to the money?
10. What did the moderator say at the end of the show?

William Conrad
Gunsmoke

Quiz #65

Match the star with his sidekick.

(Answers on page 135)

1. Phil Harris
2. Andy Brown
3. Straight Arrow
4. Beulah
5. Don Winslow
6. Helen Trent
7. Tom Mix
8. Jimmy Durante
9. Roy Rogers
10. Mr. Chameleon

a. The Kingfish
b. Frankie Remley
c. Mike Shaw
d. Gabby Hayes
e. Garry Moore
f. Oriole
g. Red Pennington
h. David Arnold
i. Agatha Anthony
j. Packy

Carlton E. Morse
Writer

Quiz #66

Multiple Choice
(Answers on page 135)

1. Boxing announcer Don Dunphy's color man was
   a) Clem McCarthy b) Bill Corum c) Howard Cosell

2. Call letters CX4 is associated with what program?
   a) Hope Harrigan b) Sky King c) Captain Midnight

3. Candy Candido appeared on what show?
   a) Mel Blanc b) Jimmy Durante c) Judy Canova

4. The song "I'm Yours" was recorded by
   a) Eddie Fisher b) Don Cornell c) The Four Aces

5. Just Plain Bill lived in
   a) Hartville b) Seville c) Waterville

6. The King of Jazz was
   a) Benny Goodman b) Miles Davis c) Paul Whiteman

7. On *The Roy Rogers Show*, Gabby Hayes was replaced by
   a) Pat Buttram b) California c) Pat Brady

8. Jack Armstrong, The All-American Boy was once played by
   a) Jim Ameche b) Don Ameche c) Frank Ameche

9. Uncle Don's last name was
   a) McNeil b) Carney c) Wilson

10. Masie was played by
    a) Ann Sheridan b) Ann Blyth c) Ann Sothern

Edward G. Robinson
Big Town

Quiz #67

Match the Ed
(Answers on page 135)

1. Who married Ida?
2. Who played Rochester?
3. Who once starred in *Big Town*?
4. Who starred in *Duffy's Tavern*?
5. Who sang with Jimmy Durante?
6. Who starred in *Mr. President*?
7. Who created Mortimer Snerd?
8. Who played a good-natured clumsy guy?
9. Who was a columnist and radio show host?
10. Who was the father of Keenan?

a. Eddie Anderson
b. Edgar Bergen
c. Ed Sullivan
d. Ed Wynn
e. Eddie Jackson
f. Eddie Bracken
g. Ed Gardner
h. Edward Arnold
i. Edward G. Robinson
j. Eddie Cantor

Quiz #68

True or False
(Answers on page 136)

1. Helen Trent's arch enemy was Cynthia Swanson.
2. Harry Richman was once sponsored by Buick.
3. *Columbia Presents Corwin* featured plays by Norman Corwin.
4. *Information, Please* was a question and answer program on advice to the love lorn.
5. *Terry and the Pirates* began with a bass drum.
6. Call the Police was once a summer replacement for Amos & Andy.
7. Joyce Jordan was a lawyer.
8. Thomas Dewey once delivered a famous impersonation of newscaster, H.V. Kaltenborn.
9. H.V. Kaltenborn's initials stood for Hans Von.
10. *The Mickey Mouse* Club began on radio.

Quiz #69

The Aldrich Family
(Answers on page 136)

1. Who created the show?
2. What play did the show come from?
3. What two radio shows did The Aldrich Family get its start with?
4. Who played Henry Aldrich?
5. Who played Homer Brown?
6. Who was the long-time sponsor?
7. What was the name of Henry's sister?
8. What were the names of Henry's mother and father?
9. What did Henry's father do for a living?
10. Who was Henry's girlfriend?

Quiz #70

Al Jolson
(Answers on page 136)

1. What was Al Jolson's real name?
2. The Kraft Music Hall was Al's last radio show. What was his first?
3. Who was Al's announcer on the Kraft Music Hall?
4. Who was the pianist on the Kraft Music Hall?
5. Name the two movies on Al's life?
6. Who played Al in both movies?
7. What was Al's theme song?
8. Who was Lou Bring?
9. Al always got down on one knee when he sang what song?
10. Al appeared in the first motion picture with sound. Name the movie.

ANSWERS

Quiz #1 *(from page 1)*
1. d
2. e
3. h
4. c
5. a
6. i
7. j
8. g
9. b
10. f

Quiz #2 *(from page 3)*
1. e
2. d
3. g
4. f
5. c
6. j
7. b
8. i
9. a
10. h

Quiz #3 *(from page 5)*
Radio – Your Hit Parade
1. Frank Sinatra
2. Andy Russell
3. Doris Day
4. Dinah Shore
5. Joan Edwards

Television – Your Hit Parade
1. Snooky Lanson
2. Dorothy Collins
3. Tommy Leonetti
4. Giselle McKenzie
5. Russell Arms

Neither
1. Eddie Fisher
2. Patti Page
3. Frankie Laine
4. Dick Haymes
5. Kitty Kallen

Quiz #4 *(from page 7)*
1. Jello
2. Wildroot Cream Oil
3. Pabst Blue Ribbon
4. Shredded Ralston
5. Duz
6. Pepto Bismol
7. Phillip Morris
8. Pepsi Cola
9. Lifeboy
10. Fitch Shampoo

Quiz #5 *(from page 9)*
1. Mr. Kitzel (Artie Auerbach)
2. Bob Crosby
3. May Company
4. Kenny Baker
5. The Sportsmen Quartet
6. Ed the guard
7. Professor LeBlanc (Mel Blanc)
8. Maxwell
9. Eddie Anderson
10. Jello and Lucky Strike

Quiz #6 *(from page 11)*
1. f
2. a
3. h
4. c
5. g
6. j
7. i
8. d
9. e
10. b

Quiz #7 *(from page 12)*
1. b
2. d
3. j
4. a
5. i
6. f
7. c
8. e
9. h
10. g

Quiz #8　*(from page 13)*
1. False (it was a popular television show)
2. False (they were two separate shows)
3. True
4. True
5. False
6. FAlse
7. True
8. False (they were made popular by President Franklin Delano Roosevelt)
9. True
10. False (it was Colgate

Quiz #9　*(from page 15)*
1. Marion and Jim Jordan
2. Johnson's Wax
3. Mayor La Trivia
4. Gale Gordon
5. Dr. Gamble
6. The Hall Closet
7. Wallace
8. Sweetie Face, my big old wife!
9. Teeny
10. Marion Jordan

Quiz #10　*(from page 17)*
1. c
2. e
3. i
4. a
5. g
6. j
7. h
8. b
9. f
10. d

Quiz #11   *(from page 19)*
1. Monday
2. Sunday
3. Friday
4. Sunday
5. Tuesday
6. Wednesday
7. Monday, Wednesday and Friday
8. Thursday
9. Sunday
10. Sunday

Quiz #12   *(from page 21)*
1. g
2. h
3. b
4. a
5. j
6. e
7. d
8. i
9. f
10. c

Quiz #13   *(from page 23)*
1. Bobby Benson
2. Bill Stern
3. The adopted son of Nick Carter.
4. Irene Wicker
5. Johnny
6. Lou Holtz
7. He was a counterspy.
8. Judy Price
9. First Nighter
10. Gangbusters

Quiz #14 *(from page 24)*

1. Brace Beamer
2. John Reid
3. John Todd
4. Dan Reid
5. There were six state rangers. All were ambushed and five were killed. The sixth was the lone survivor and took the name, The Lone Ranger.
6. The Butch Cavandish Gang
7. Cheerios
8. A silver bullet
9. Heigh-Yo, Silver!
10. Faithful Friend

Quiz #15 *(from page 25)*

1. Colgate
2. Campbells' Soups
3. Halo
4. Chevrolet
5. Anacin
6. Ivory Soap
7. Cheerios
8. Kellogg's Pep
9. Nestlees
10. Wheaties

Quiz #16 *(from page 27)*

1. False (the role of Tom Mix was played by Curley Bradley)
2. True
3. True
4. True
5. False (he played for Al Jolson)
6. False (it's only star was Fannie Brice)
7. False (it was never on radio)
8. True
9. False
10. True

Quiz #17 *(from page 29)*

1. j
2. h
3. b
4. a
5. e
6. f
7. d
8. i
9. c
10. g

Quiz #18 *(from page 30)*

1. Freeman Gosden and Charles Correll
2. George Stevens
3. The Mystic Knights of the Sea
4. Freeman Gosden
5. Sapphire
6. He owned the Fresh Air Taxi Company
7. Madam Queen
8. "Baldy!"
9. Algonquin J. Calhoun (originally it was Stonewall)
10. Lightnin'

Quiz #19 *(from page 31)*

1. h
2. i
3. b
4. e
5. j
6. c
7. f
8. a
9. g
10. d

Quiz #20 *(from page 33)*

1. b
2. d
3. i
4. e
5. a
6. j
7. f
8. c
9. h
10. g

Quiz #21 *(from page 35)*

1. He gave advice to people with problems. He was the Dear Abby of radio.
2. Carlton E. Morse
3. *Inner Sanctum*
4. The panelists on *It Pays to be Ignorant*
5. Arthur Treacher
6. The Goldbergs
7. Life Can Be Beautiful
8. Lum Edwards and Abner Peabody
9. The Jot 'em Down Store
10. Pine Ridge, Arkansas

Quiz #22 *(from page 37)*

1. b
2. d
3. g
4. i
5. f
6. j
7. a
8. h
9. c
10. e

Quiz #23 *(from page 38)*
1. Lamont Cranston
2. Margo Laine
3. He had the ability to cloud men's minds.
4. In the Orient
5. Years ago
6. Orson Welles
7. Commissioner Weston
8. Shrevie
9. Blue Coal
10. "Who knows what evil lurks in the hearts of men…!"

Quiz #24 *(from page 39)*
1. trombone
2. clarinet
3. trumpet
4. drums
5. saxophone
6. trombone
7. violin
8. guitar
9. piano
10. saxophone

Quiz #25 *(from page 41)*
1. True
2. False (*The Romance of Helen Trent* preceded *Our Gal Sunday*)
3. False (he appeared on *Vic and Sade*)
4. True
5. False (it was her sister Rosemary)
6. True
7. True
8. True
9. False (she starred in *Stella Dallas*)
10. False (her name was Belle)

Quiz #26 *(from page 43)*
1. j
2. a
3. i
4. d
5. g
6. c
7. h
8. e
9. b
10. f

Quiz #27 *(from page 45)*
1. d
2. f
3. i
4. e
5. a
6. c
7. b
8. g
9. j
10. h

Quiz #28 *(from page 47)*
1. Winston
2. Ballantine
3. Ipana
4. Sal Hapatica
5. Pepsodent
6. Lipton Tea
7. Cool
8. Lustre Crème Shampoo
9. Ajax
10. Blue Bonnett

Quiz #29   *(from page 48)*

1. c
2. f
3. e
4. g
5. a
6. b
7. i
8. j
9. h
10. d

Quiz #30   *(from page 49)*

1. Fibber McGee and Molly
2. Harold Peary
3. Willard Waterman
4. Throckmorton P. Gildersleeve
5. Marjorie and Leroy
6. "Unk"
7. Birdie
8. Parkay Margerine
9. Peavey
10. Horace Hooker

Quiz #31   *(from page 51)*

1. j
2. f
3. g
4. b
5. i
6. d
7. a
8. c
9. h
10. e

Quiz #32   *(from page 53)*
1.   The Tracer of Lost Persons
2.   Mike Clancy
3.   Effie
4.   "Sam Spade Detective Agency"
5.   Mr. Chameleon
6.   Jack Webb
7.   Dragnet
8.   He sang a song.
9.   Mr. District Attorney
10. Harrington

Quiz #33   *(from page 55)*
1.   On a drug store scale
2.   Brad Runyan
3.   Nick Charles
4.   Nora Charles
5.   Dashiell Hammett
6.   J. Scott Smart
7.   A harp
8.   Peptol Bismol
9.   Asta
10. Post Toasties

Quiz #34   *(from page 57)*
1.   h
2.   j
3.   d
4.   b
5.   c
6.   e
7.   a
8.   f
9.   g
10. i

Quiz #35 *(from page 58)*

1. True
2. False (Jackie Gleason was the first Riley on television)
3. True
4. True
5. False (they sang with Roy Rogers)
6. True
7. False (he played the accordion)
8. False (the sponsor was Waterman Pens)
9. False (it was created by Abbott and Costello)
10. False (he appeared on *Fibber McGee & Molly*)

Quiz #36 *(from page 59)*

1. c
2. a
3. h
4. i
5. d
6. j
7. b
8. f
9. e
10. g

Quiz #37 *(from page 60)*

1. Britt Reid
2. He was the owner as well as the editor of the newspaper, *The Daily Sentinal.*
3. Lenore Kace
4. A hornet seal from his ring
5. Black Beauty
6. Kato
7. He was Phillipino
8. Michael Axford
9. The Flight of the Bumblebee
10. "Extra, extra, read all about it!"

Quiz #38   *(from page 61)*

1. c
2. e
3. h
4. a
5. j
6. g
7. b
8. i
9. d
10. f

Quiz #39   *(from page 63)*

1. j
2. c
3. g
4. d
5. i
6. a
7. f
8. h
9. e
10. b

Quiz #40   *(from page 64)*

1. She owned a lumber yard.
2. He was a barber.
3. When a Girl Marries
4. Silver Creek, Colorado
5. Producers and writers of many soap operas
6. Gil Whitney
7. Lorenzo Jones
8. She was a lawyer.
9. Aunt Jenney
10. Perry

Quiz #41 *(from page 65)*

1. e
2. d
3. a
4. h
5. b
6. j
7. g
8. i
9. f
10. c

Quiz #42 *(from page 67)*

1. Shaeffer
2. Ovaltine
3. Marlboro
4. Brill Crème
5. Bromo Seltzer
6. Lucky Strike
7. Tetley Tea
8. Tide's
9. Spic and Span
10. Nabisco Shredded Wheat

Quiz #43 *(from page 69)*

1. j
2. i
3. e
4. b
5. a
6. g
7. f
8. c
9. d
10. h

Quiz #44 *(from page 71)*

1. a
2. d
3. e
4. b
5. j
6. h
7. f
8. c
9. g
10. i

Quiz #45 *(from page 72)*

1. Fannie Brice
2. Frank Morgan
3. *Maxwell House Coffee Time*
4. Higgins
5. Hanley Stafford
6. Lancelot Higgins
7. Vera Higgins
8. Robespierre
9. He spoke all jumbled up. Snooks was the only person who could understand him!
10. Rock A Bye Baby

Quiz #46 *(from page 73)*

1. James Melton
2. Carmen Lombardo
3. Kenny Gardner
4. Tommy Dorsey and Harry James
5. The Pennsylvanians
6. Arthur Tracy
7. Stop the Music
8. Kay Armen
9. The Happiness Boys
10. Phil Harris

Quiz #47 *(from page 75)*
1. Monday
2. Sunday
3. Wednesday
4. Tuesday
5. Thursday
6. Tuesday and Thursday
7. Sunday
8. Monday
9. Tuesday
10. Monday

Quiz #48 *(from page 76)*
1. h
2. j
3. c
4. g
5. b
6. e
7. d
8. f
9. i
10. a

Quiz #49 *(from page 77)*
1. Bud Collier
2. The planet of Krypton
3. Kryptonyte
4. The Daily Planet
5. Perry White
6. Lois Lane
7. Jimmy Olson
8. A locomotive
9. Kellogg's Pep
10. In a phone booth

Quiz #50   *(from page 79)*
1. e
2. g
3. f
4. d
5. a
6. j
7. b
8. h
9. i
10. c

Quiz #51   *(from page 81)*
1. True
2. True
3. False (it was Miss Miller)
4. True
5. False (it was Major Edward Bowes)
6. False (it was Mayor Fiorello LaGuardia)
7. True
8. True
9. False (they only appeared on television)
10. True

Quiz #52   *(from page 83)*
1. *The Romance of Helen Trent*
2. *Our Gal Sunday*
3. *Mary Noble, Backstage Wife*
4. *Stella Dallas*
5. *One Man's Family*
6. *When a Girl Marries*
7. *Lorenzo Jones and His Wife Belle*
8. *Life Can Be Beautiful*

Quiz #53 *(from page 84)*
1. h
2. d
3. j
4. c
5. f
6. g
7. i
8. a
9. b
10. e

Quiz #54 *(from page 85)*
1. Longines
2. Barbasol
3. Super Suds
4. Fatima
5. Royal Pudding
6. Bulova
7. Maxwell House
8. Chock Full of Nuts
9. Doublemint Gum
10. Pall Mall

Quiz #55 *(from page 87)*
1. b
2. d
3. f
4. a
5. i
6. h
7. j
8. c
9. e
10. g

Quiz #56 *(from page 89)*
1. a
2. c
3. a
4. b
5. b
6. a
7. c
8. b
9. c
10. c

Quiz #57 *(from page 91)*
1. j
2. i
3. g
4. e
5. d
6. h
7. a
8. c
9. f
10. b

Quiz #58 *(from page 92)*
1. Eve Arden
2. Connie
3. Madison High School
4. English
5. Mr. Boynton
6. Biology
7. Jeff Chandler
8. Osgood Conklin
9. Gale Gordon
10. Mrs. Davis

Quiz #59 *(from page 93)*
1. a
2. f
3. g
4. b
5. i
6. e
7. c
8. d
9. j
10. h

Quiz #60 *(from page 95)*
1. e
2. g
3. i
4. j
5. d
6. c
7. a
8. f
9. b
10. h

Quiz #61 *(from page 97)*
1. The Whistler
2. Fibber McGee & Molly
3. The Green Hornet
4. Inner Sanctum
5. Truth or Consequences
6. Duffy's Tavern
7. Boston Blackie
8. Breakfast Clubbers
9. Escape
10. Suspense

Quiz #62 *(from page 99)*

1. b
2. d
3. c
4. f
5. h
6. a
7. i
8. e
9. g
10. j

Quiz #63 *(from page 101)*

1. h
2. d
3. c
4. i
5. a
6. g
7. f
8. j
9. e
10. b

Quiz #64 *(from page 103)*

1. Senator Ford, Harry Hershfield, and Joe Laurie, Jr.
2. Senator Ford – "Good Evening"; Harry Hershfield – "Howdy"; Joe Laurie, Jr. – "Hello"
3. Senator Ford
4. Ward Wilson
5. Peter Donald
6. The Laugh Meter
7. 1000
8. $25
9. A recording of Peter Donald telling his joke on the air
10. "...Until then, we remain yours for bigger and better laughs!"

Quiz #65 *(from page 105)*
1. b
2. a
3. j
4. f
5. g
6. i
7. c
8. e
9. d
10. h

Quiz #66 *(from page 107)*
1. b
2. a
3. b
4. all three
5. a
6. c
7. c
8. a
9. b
10. c

Quiz #67 *(from page 109)*
1. j
2. a
3. i
4. g
5. e
6. h
7. b
8. f
9. c
10. d

Quiz #68 *(from page 110)*

1. True
2. False (it was Dodge)
3. True
4. False (it was a quiz show)
5. False (it began with a gong)
6. True
7. False (she was a doctor)
8. False (it was President Harry Truman)
9. True
10. False (only on television)

Quiz #69 *(from page 111)*

1. Clifford Goldsmith
2. What a Life
3. Rudy Vallee and Kate Smith
4. Ezra Stone
5. Jackie Kelk
6. Jello
7. Mary
8. Alice and Sam
9. He was a lawyer
10. Agnes Lawson

Quiz #70 *(from page 112)*

1. Asa Yoelson
2. Shell Chateau
3. Ken Carpenter
4. Oscar Levant
5. The Jolson Story and Jolson Sings Again
6. Larry Parks
7. April Showers
8. Al's orchestra leader on the Kraft Music Hall
9. Mammy
10. The Jazz Singer

Printed in the United States
22704LVS00004B/427-483